OFF TO THE RACES

PETER & NILDA SESSLER

The Rourke Press, Inc.
Vero Beach, Florida 32964

© 1999 The Rourke Press, Inc.

PHOTO CREDITS
© Indianapolis Motor Speedway: cover, pages 6, 7, 12, 16, 19; © Infinity Motorsports: pages 4, 13, 18, 21; © Oldsmobile: pages 10, 15, 22; © Peter Sessler: page 9

EDITORIAL SERVICES:
Susan Albury

Library of Congress Cataloging-in-Publication Data

Sessler, Peter C., 1950-
  Indy cars / Peter Sessler, Nilda Sessler.
    p. cm. — (Off to the races)
  Includes index.
  Summary: Describes the small but powerful cars that race in the Indianapolis 500, their sponsorship, and racing rules.
    ISBN 1-57103-281-9
  1. Indy cars Juvenile literature. 2. Indianapolis Speedway Race Juvenile literature. [1. Indy cars. 2. Indianapolis Speedway Race. 3. Automobiles, Racing.] I. Sessler, Nilda, 1951- . II. Title. III. Series: Sessler, Peter C., 1950- Off to the races.
GV1033.5.I55S47 1999
796.72—dc21   99-13823
                                                                      CIP

Printed in the USA

■■ TABLE OF CONTENTS

THE HISTORY OF INDY RACING

The first Indianapolis 500 race was held in 1911. The winner drove his car at an average speed of 74.6 miles per hour (mph). Today, the fastest Indy cars can average over 235 miles per hour!

 The tires on the first Indy racers were made of solid rubber.

The race at Indianapolis has a long history, and today it is still America's best-known race.

The most popular car race in the world happens every year on Memorial Day weekend at Indianapolis, Indiana. Thirty-three cars compete in a 200-lap (500-mile) long race at the Indianapolis Motor Speedway. Over 300,000 people watch from the stands and millions more watch the race on TV. It is truly a national event.

Indy cars have changed in the past 60 years. A mechanic used to ride with the driver during the race! The track at Indianapolis is sometimes called the Brickyard, because it used to be covered with bricks.

Over 300,000 people watch the Indy 500 race on Memorial Day every year.

Indy cars were first developed for the Indianapolis 500, but now they also race at other tracks around the country and around the world.

▨ INDY RACING RULES

There are two groups that make the rules for the Indy-type racecars and they are called the sanctioning bodies. They are the IRL (Indy Racing League) and CART (Championship Auto Racing Teams). As sanctioning bodies, for example, they say how long the cars can be, how much they must weigh, how big the engines can be, and many other rules.

In this way, all cars will be as equal as possible. Sometimes all these rules together are known as a formula. In Europe, cars similar to the Indy cars are called formula cars.

There are rules about everything in racing. How wide the tires can be, how big the wings can be, and, most important, how big the engine can be are a few examples.

♟ A WORD FROM OUR SPONSOR

It can cost over $25 million to run a team for a year. So companies, like Crest toothpaste, help to pay the cost of running the team and are called **sponsors** (SPON sirz). Sponsors can put their company name or logo on the car and driver's uniform. Companies that pay more get to have larger logos on the car.

 A. J. Foyt is the only driver who has won the Indy 500 four times: 1961, 1964, 1967, 1977

All Indy race cars are covered with the stickers and logos of the companies that sponsor the car. Even the driver's suits have logos on them.

◼️◻️◼️ THE TRACK

IRL cars race mostly on oval tracks that are located in different parts of the country. The best-known oval track is in Indianapolis. Cars racing under CART rules race on oval tracks and also race on road courses. They even race on city streets. Road courses have many tight and twisty curves as well as **straightaways** (STRATE ah wayz).

This is the famous Indianapolis Speedway. It is a rectangular oval track. The track is 2-1/2 miles long.

One of the reasons why Indy cars can go so fast is the banked or tilted turns of the track. The cars almost glide around the turns.

Each track has a garage area where the mechanics work on the cars and **pits** (PITZ), where cars stop during a race to get more fuel or have tires changed.

◼️◻️ THE INCREDIBLE CARS

Indy-type cars are powerful but light, weighing around 1,500 pounds. Their engines can **generate** (JEN ur rate) about 1,200 horsepower. Cars in the IRL use engines made by Oldsmobile and Infiniti, while those that race in CART use engines made by Mercedes, Honda, and Ford.

Gasoline Alley is the name given for the garage area at Indianapolis Speedway.

Today's Indy cars are very complex. To win races you have to have a good running car and also a very good driver.

The driver's seat is inside the part of the car called a "tub" with the front **suspension** (suh SPEN shun) attached to the front of the tub. In the rear, behind the driver's seat is the engine and transmission. The gas tanks are located along the sides of the car. Indy cars do not use gasoline. Instead, they use a type of alcohol called **methanol** (METH ah nall) as fuel.

Indy cars are so powerful and fast, that there are many rules to make sure the driver is safe in case of an accident. All drivers have to wear special fireproof suits and special helmets. The area around the driver's seat is made extra strong and drivers are strapped in with special belts.

The race cars are small and very powerful. Front and rear wings are needed to keep the car close to the ground at high speeds.

THE RACE IS ON!

The cars always arrive at the track several days before the race. This way, drivers get a chance to practice on the track. Meanwhile, mechanics go over the cars to make sure they are working properly. They also make adjustments so the cars drive safely and quickly.

All the race teams take many practice laps to make sure the cars run perfectly. Here a mechanic is making an adjustment to the engine.

Each team has a highly trained pit crew. The faster the pit crew changes the tires and fills the gas tank, the sooner the car can get back in the race.

At Indianapolis, each driver must drive his car as fast as possible for four laps. These are called **qualifying** (KWA la fie ing) laps. The fastest three cars then start on the first row, the second fastest three cars on the second row, until all 11 rows are filled.

On race day, a pace car slowly leads all the cars around the track. If everything is okay, the pace car pulls off the track and the starter waves the green flag. The race is on!

During a long race, the cars have to come into the pits to get more fuel and have their tires changed. They may also come into the pits if the car is having a problem or needs repairs.

When the checkered flag is waved at the leading car, the race is over. The winning driver gets a trophy and prize money. After the race, all the teams go to the next track to race once again.

At the end of the year, the driver who has won the most races becomes champion.

The fastest Indy cars can go over 250 mph.

The green flag is given and the cars zoom off! The pole on the right shows the position of each car during the race.

GLOSSARY

generate (JEN ur rate) — to make or to produce

methanol (METH ah nall) — a clear, poisonous, liquid alcohol used in fuel

qualifying (KWA la fie ing) — a way to get the best starting position

pits (PITZ) — any area alongside an auto racecourse used for refueling and repairing the cars during a race

sponsors (SPON sirz) — a company that helps pay for a racing team

straightaways (STRATE ah wayz) — the straight part of a closed racecourse

suspension (suh SPEN shun) — the system of devices supporting the upper part of the vehicle

CONVERSION TABLE

74.6 miles per hour .120 kilometers per hour	1,500 pounds............................680 kilograms
500 miles.................................805 kilometers	250 miles per hour ..403 kilometers per hour

It is a happy time for Eddie Cheever, the winner of the 1997 and 1998 Indy 500 races.

■ INDEX

FURTHER READING

Find out more about racing with these helpful books and organizations:

• David Rubel, *How to Drive an Indy Race Car (Masters of Motion)*. 1992

• Rick Popely & The Editors of Consumer Guide, *Indianapolis 500 Chronicle*. 1998
  The book covers the exciting history of the Indy 500 race since 1911.

• *Indy Review '98*
  This is the official publication of the Indianapolis Motor Speedway

• IRL's Official Site: www.indyracingleague.com

• CART's Official Site: www.cart.com

• www.goracing.com
  Lots of information on all types of racing. The site also posts the results of every race.